Funny Things That Happened on the Way to Heaven

by

Anthony F. Rigoli, O.M.I.

authorHOUSE™

1663 LIBERTY DRIVE, SUITE 200
BLOOMINGTON, INDIANA 47403
(800) 839-8640
WWW.AUTHORHOUSE.COM

First published by AuthorHouse 11/05/04

ISBN: 1-4184-9998-6 (sc)

Printed in the United States of America
Bloomington, Indiana

This book is printed on acid-free paper.

ACKNOWLEDGEMENTS

I wish to thank everyone who encouraged me to put into writing the many funny things that have occurred in my life as a priest. A special word of thanks to Fran Schmidt from D'Youville College and to Sr. Carol Ann Kleindinst, SSMN, for proof reading and typing and to Jane Killewald. Above all, a special thanks to the many people who help put smiles on our faces each day.

DEDICATION

Finally, I want to dedicate this book to my Mom. She taught me that laughter is truly a gift and a blessing. My Mom died last year. She had Alzheimer's, but we continued to laugh each day that we were together. Her sense of humor and her ability to make us laugh were her greatest gifts to me and to my family.

Table of Contents

DOES GOD HAVE A SENSE OF HUMOR?

How often that question has come up in discussions from Bible Studies or from people just sharing their faith! Does God have a sense of humor?

For years, friends and relatives have told me I should write a book about funny things that have happened throughout my life as a priest. These events have kept my life from being anything but boring. Most of these moments have taken place over the past 32 years that I have been a priest.

All of us are on a journey. This journey leads us to heaven. Along the way, each of us have encountered funny and interesting things that make our life exciting and full of laughs.

In this small book, I hope to capture some of the funny things that have happened to me on my journey to heaven. I have changed the names to protect the "innocent".

I truly hope this book helps you to reflect on the funny things that have happened to you during your lifetime. I believe everyone needs to laugh more. Laughter is the key to a healthy life. I have often said that in life we need three bones to have happiness:

> *We need a Wish Bone. We need to have dreams. I really like dreamers. We need a Back Bone. We need to be strong to achieve our dreams and goals but most importantly,*

we need a Funny Bone. We need to laugh at
ourselves more often.

Jesus, I am convinced, must have laughed with his friends. I am certain that Peter must have put a smile on his face many times.

Finally, I want to dedicate this book to my Mom. She taught me that laughter is truly a gift and a blessing. My Mom died last year. She had Alzheimer's, but we continued to laugh each day that we were together. Her sense of humor and her ability to make us laugh were her greatest gifts to me and to my family.

(All Scriptures passages are taken from The New American Bible)

"JOY IS THE ECHO OF GOD'S LIFE

WITHIN US"

-St. Ireneus

Anthony F. Rigoli, O.M.I.

THE ANOINTING

It was a typical wintry evening in Buffalo. The call came into the rectory around one in the morning from the Intensive Care Unit at Erie County Medical Center. A woman was requesting that a priest come to anoint her husband who wasn't doing very well.

When I arrived at the hospital, I immediately headed to the ICU. As I entered the room, the patient was not only surprised by my presence, but also seemed agitated. As I prayed with him, he became much more disturbed. Since he had a feeding tube, he was unable to communicate with me. I felt badly since he was not at all at peace by my being with him.

As I was leaving the room, the nurse came from the nurses' station, and said that she was sure that the man I had anointed appreciated the visit, but I had the wrong room. I had just anointed the wrong man. His name was Mr. Goldstein.

She directed me to the correct room and there was a woman with her husband in a coma. As I related the story to her, she couldn't stop laughing. She told me this was the first time she had smiled in a while. She was very appreciative. I guess there was a reason for the mistaken anointing. By the way, both Mr. Goldstein and the other patient went home eventually. I wonder if Mr. Goldstein remembers the blessing!

"MY BEING PROCLAIMS THE GREATNESS OF THE LORD, MY SPIRIT FINDS JOY IN GOD MY SAVIOR"

——*from Mary's Magnificat*

Anthony F. Rigoli, O.M.I.

ALLELUIA AS SIGN LANGUAGE

Again, it was my first year as a priest, and I was assigned to a parish where we had a monthly Mass in sign language. There were a number of parishioners who were deaf. Prior to this assignment, I had taken several years of sign language. Truthfully, if you don't use it daily, you will forget it very easily.

During the first Mass that I was to sign, I must admit I was very nervous. I had practiced my signs and hoped not to make too much of a mess of things.

All was going well until it came to the Alleluia before the Gospel. I placed my thumb between my fingers and instead of swinging my hand above my head in jubilee; I did the same sign under my ear. Well, the deaf community all began to laugh. I was signing very excitedly, although it wasn't the sign for Alleluia, but for "I have to use the restroom". Oh, how patient they were with me, but I knew they couldn't wait to see what would come next.

*"REJOICE IN THE LORD ALWAYS,
AGAIN, I SAY REJOICE"*

Anthony F. Rigoli, O.M.I.

CONFIRMATION

Several years ago, I had a wonderful group of young high school students for confirmation class at Holy Angels' Parish in Buffalo, N.Y. One of the young men was the quarterback for Grover Cleveland High School. The team that year was in the playoff, and unfortunately, Confirmation was scheduled on the very Saturday of the playoffs. Jeff certainly was a dedicated Catholic, but was also a valuable player on his team. He told me that the game began at noon, and Confirmation wasn't until four in the afternoon. Well, as things go, the game went into overtime. As the Mass began, Jeff was nowhere in sight. However, ten minutes after the ceremony began, in came Jeff, dressed and muddy in his football uniform with his sponsor following behind him. It was quite a sight. Bishop McLaughlin, much to everyone's delight, spoke out, "Tell me, Jeff, did we win?" When he said, "Yes". The entire congregation cheered. I think we learned a lot about the meaning of commitment that Confirmation Day. For sure, Jeff was a sign to his teammates as well as his confirmation class about his love for the Church.

*"I HAVE COME THAT YOUR JOY MAY
BE COMPLETE"*

Anthony F. Rigoli, O.M.I.

CAN YOU LAUGH ON GOOD FRIDAY?

Growing up in an Italian family, we had our special customs and traditions. One such custom was on Good Friday from noon until three in the afternoon. In our neighborhood on the West Side of Buffalo, almost everyone was Italian, and, naturally, Catholic. We had an unwritten rule that during those sacred hours on Good Friday, you didn't play outside, and there were neither radios nor television during those hours. Those were hours to remember what Jesus did for each of us.

One thing that did occur during those hours was that my Mom would be making her special Easter cookies. They were called in English 'eggs in a basket'. They were huge cookies with a hard-boiled egg in them. Not only did my Mom make those Easter delights, but also pretty much most of the neighbors on old York Street did the same. They would be given to each child along with the usual Easter chocolate on Easter Sunday.

I always remember one woman in our neighborhood. I used to call her the 'Good Friday Lady'. She always wore black. Someone from the old country probably died twenty years ago and she was still mourning. She never smiled, but I must say, she seemed a little more cheery on Good Friday. I guess she identified with the cross and felt good about it.

When I was ordained, I was given the task of being the narrator for the reading of the long Passion that is read on

Good Friday. It is the Gospel where we stand for quite some time. As I was reading, the line was to be read,"And they came for Jesus in the garden, and Peter took out the sword and cut off the servant's ear." Well, I missed the line and with much vigor I read: "He took out the sword and cut off the servant's Peter". Well, the house came down. To this day, I still become a little nervous every Good Friday when I have to read the Passion.

By the way, we had the largest crowd on Easter to see whatever happened to Peter!

Anthony F. Rigoli, O.M.I.

"I BRING GOOD TIDINGS OF GREAT JOY, A JOY TO BE SHARED BY THE WHOLE PEOPLE".

THE CAR WASH

It was my first year as a priest, and I had been assigned to St. Margaret Mary Parish in Harrisburg, Pennsylvania. It was Valentine's Day and as I was about ready to leave the rectory to visit parishioners in the hospital, the pastor, Fr. Casey, reminded me to pick up some candy for the women who worked in the rectory. After my visit to the hospital, I ran into a nearby drugstore to pick up several boxes of candy. As I was getting into my car, I noticed there was a car wash next to the drugstore. They were running a special wax and wash for the same price.

Immediately, I got in line to get my car washed. However, as the pulley moved my care along through the car wash, I had forgotten one thing. The back window was wide open. Here I was in the middle of this car wash, getting totally soaked. I finally managed to get the back window up. I got washed and waxed as well as the car.

The candy, by the way, *was a little soaked*. Never again will I forget Valentine's Day.

"A JOYFUL HEART IS THE HEALTH OF THE BODY BUT A DEPRESSED SPIRIT DRIES UP THE BONES".

Proverbs 17:21-22

MARRYING THE DEAD

While assigned to St. Jude's Parish in Sumter, South Carolina, I had been helping a couple prepare to have their marriage blessed in the Church. They had been married civilly for several years and had two young sons. The husband was much older, and had been retired from the Navy. One evening I received a call from the hospital that he had a heart attack, and was in the emergency room. I rushed to the hospital, but it was too late. His wife, in distress, reminded me that she wanted to have their marriage blessed. She insisted that I bless their marriage. Since she was in such a state, I said a prayer for them as she held his hand. To this day, many ask if I still marry the dead. She had announced at the funeral that I had married them in the hospital.

Continuing with this couple, the man had in his Will that he wanted to be buried at sea, since he had spent his life in the Navy. Well, there was much debate between his wife and his family. She asked me,' Do you think he will be wet?" The real clincher was when she asked, "Where do you think I should tell the boys where their Daddy is buried when they want to go see his grave?" I didn't say this, but I thought, "Just turn on the faucet and say, 'Let's say a prayer for Daddy!'".

Anthony F. Rigoli, O.M.I.

"Make me a Channel of your peace. Where there is despair in life, let me bring hope. Where there is darkness only light, and where there is sadness ever joy".

St. Francis of Assisi

REALLY, OH, THAT'S TOO BAD

During my years spent in the small town of Watervliet, New York, I would often visit the sick at Samaritan Hospital in nearby Troy, New York. On this one particular day, I had gone to visit a parishioner from the parish where I would assist at on weekends. As I came off the elevator onto the fourth floor, a nurse approached me if I could speak Italian. I kindly told her that I could understand Italian but was not fluent in speaking the language. She went on to tell me that there was a patient on the floor who had been asking for a priest. He spoke no English.

Well, I gave it my best try. I went to his room with the nurse, and he was happy to see me, and immediately starting speaking in a dialect with which I was not familiar. He went on for about twenty minutes. I have to be honest. I did not understand one word. I knew he was making his confession. I kept on saying in Italian, "Oh, really?" and "That's too bad." For all I know, he may have murdered his wife. But I did know that he was getting whatever he needed off his chest and heart. Afterwards, I gave him absolution and Holy Communion. He seemed to be in such peace.

The following day, I returned to the hospital to visit parishioners. As I was passing by the room of this man, I noticed the room was empty. I went to the nurse's station and inquired about the man. The nurse told me that about thirty minutes after I had left him, he died so peacefully with a smile on his face. Who can call this a coincidence?

I rejoice heartily in the Lord,

in my God is the joy of my soul".

—*Isaiah*

Anthony F. Rigoli, O.M.I.

TRUSTING IN THE LORD

This is another Good Samaritan story. Once again, has to deal with car problems. It was the month of January, and I was returning from a trip back into Buffalo. It was around midnight, and I went to start my car that had been parked at the airport. I knew there was something wrong when I started the engine. I was able to get out of the parking lot and onto the highway, but about two miles later, beneath the underpass, the car just died. It was the alternator. It was freezing outdoors, and my hope was that some kind person would see me and give me a lift to the next exit. Then I could call the rectory and get one of my fellow priests to pick me up.

Time passed, and all of a sudden, an old beat-up car pulled beside me. There were three young men in the car. At first sight, I thought they looked like thugs. They asked me if they could be of help. My first thought was "Well, if they rob me, at least I will be out of the cold for a bit and in a warm car." I told them, "Just take me to the next exit." They insisted on taking me to my destination. At this point, they didn't know that I was a priest. I told them I worked at D'Youville College and lived next to the college. I didn't know if they would know where it was located. Well, the driver immediately told me that his brother attended the college and he took him to classes each day in order to use the car. He knew the short cut to the school, and when I offered them money, they said it was their pleasure. I always feel God watches over children, the handicapped and Fr. Tony. This proves it.

"The best sign of indwelling grace is spiritual joy. The heart that is free and joyful with good will is better disposed for the reception of grace than the heart that is fettered with sadness and bitterness."

——*St. Bonaventure*

Anthony F. Rigoli, O.M.I.

HOSTAGE IN SOUTH CAROLINA

Not all of my stories are funny. Some of my life experiences were actually sad. One such story was on August 25, 1984 in Sumter, South Carolina. It started off as a normal day. However, by around 9 o'clock, a man whom I had counseled the day before returned to ask to use the telephone. He wanted to call his wife who had left him. He wanted to see his children. She told him she would call him back, but she never did, and he left the office. Several hours later, he appeared again at the rectory. This time he had three of his children with him. He announced to me that he had just murdered his wife and her mother. I was really in a state of shock.

Luckily, I convinced him to let the children stay at the convent next door while I would try to talk with him. He agreed. Well, the event turned into a nightmare. He began to hold two others and me in the rectory as hostages. He told us that if we called the police or if the police showed up, he would have to kill us with the rifle he held.

Now, talk about excitement! Throughout the four-hour ordeal, he kept on asking me if I thought God would forgive him. Now, if someone is holding a rifle at you and he asked if God would forgive him, what would you say? I practically offered him a job, if he so desired!

After the four hours, he surrendered. I have kept in touch with him over all these years. Who ever said life is dull in the rectory?

Anthony F. Rigoli, O.M.I.

"The best way to progress in virtue is to preserve holy joyousness."

——*St. Philip Neri*

A GOOD SAMARITAN

While serving at St. Jude's Parish in Sumter, South Carolina, I was invited one day for dinner to the home of a family that lived on Shaw Air Force Base. When I arrived for dinner, Pete, the husband, told me that his wife had to take their daughter to the hospital for a check-up. She was nine months pregnant. While there,Sue, his wife, called from the hospital and announced that their daughter was going into labor. Peter asked me if I would accompany him to the hospital in Columbia, South Carolina, which was approximately forty-five minutes away. When we arrived, the new baby had arrived. The nurses came out and invited the immediate family in to see the baby. Since I was with them, they told the nurse I was "Father." The nurse, not hearing correctly, thought they said I was the father of the baby. Mind you, the girl was twenty-one. I am sure the nurse was puzzled. I know from her look, she must have wondered…this old man…the father!

As time went by, I needed to return to Sumter. Pete gave me his car, since his wife had the second car. I drove back, and it was around eleven o'clock in the evening by now. The highway was very dark, and all at once, I got a flat tire. Well, there I was, stranded in a foreign car. I had no idea where the spare was and I was unable to see very well because of the darkened highway. Finally, a car pulled up behind me. The gentleman got out, and seeing my distress, found that the spare was hidden under the rear of the station wagon of this foreign car. As he was helping me fix the tire, he asked me where I lived. I told him Sumter. He then asked me what I did for a living. I told him I was a Catholic priest. He couldn't stop smiling. He was a Presbyterian minister in a neighboring town. I knew that he was a Good Samaritan. We have kept in touch from that day on.

"If you have faith, preach it. If you have joy, share it.

Find the bright side of things and help others to get sight of it.

This is the only and surest way to be cheerful and happy."

——*Thomas Paine*

POOR MR.C

During my years spent at a parish in South Carolina, I can well remember the day that Mr. C died. The family were transplants from the North. Prior to his dying, his wife had asked me if I would celebrate his funeral when he died. The day after he died, she called screaming on the phone,"You'll never guess what they did to my Nick." What could they possibly have done to him, since he died? The hospital gave the undertaker the wrong man and they cremated Mr.C. She had wanted a viewing, since the family was coming down from up North. She asked me to please call the undertaker and verify what had taken place.

The undertaker was in a panic, and asked me to plead with her not to put the incident in the newspaper. He felt it would certainly ruin his business. He promised her anything she wanted for the funeral, except, of course, a viewing.

When I called her back, I wanted to say, "Mrs. C., remember Nick—just call him 'Dusty'! Of course, I didn't say that, but it did occur to me. They had quite the wake with a closed casket. She told everyone it was closed because the doctor suggested it, since they would not recognize Mr. C.

"Trust in Yahweh and do what is good, make your home in the land and live in peace. Make Yahweh your only joy and he will give you what your heart desires."

———*Psalm 37*

THE PIZZA MAN

While in South Carolina, I also taught at St. Jude High School. Every year we had a raffle to benefit the high school. This one year, I decided to raffle off making pizzas for the lucky winner.

The family that won the prize asked if I could make the pizzas for their annual family reunion that was coming up in the next month. I agreed and the afternoon of the reunion, I made four sheet pizzas. I put on my special pizza hat and drove off to the picnic area where the family was gathered. When I arrived many children saw the car drive up and immediately spotted the hat and yelled, "The pizza man is here! The pizza man is here!" Little did they know that it was Padre's Pizza. They were shocked to realize that a priest had made the pizza.

"Happy the one who puts their trust in Yahweh"

——Psalm 40

Anthony F. Rigoli, O.M.I.

THE GROOM IN THE BATHROOM

At present, I am the Campus Minister at D'Youville College in Buffalo, New York. I really enjoy my work with college students. After they graduate, many keep in contact and have asked if I would celebrate their marriages.

One couple was going to be married in the chapel at the University of Rochester, and I drove to Rochester that morning. As we were waiting in a side room with the very excited groom and his best man, the groom asked me if I had any funny things that ever happened at weddings. I recounted many incidents and told him I would like to write a book about funny things that have happened at weddings.

It was about two minutes before the ceremony was to begin, and the young groom wanted to use the restroom. Lo and behold, as he tried to get out of the room, the door was locked with him inside. It didn't take long to get him out, but by the way he was in a tremendous state of panic. I couldn't stop laughing and smiling throughout the ceremony. This was definitely one for the wedding book.

"Do not abandon yourself to sorrow, do not torment yourself with brooding. Gladness of heart is life to one, joy is what gives us strength of days."

——Book of Ecclesiasticus

Anthony F. Rigoli, O.M.I.

VIETNAMESE WEDDING

While assigned to Holy Angels Parish, there were a number of Vietnamese families in the parish. Whenever we had a Vietnamese wedding, I was fortunate to have an interpreter to assist with the ceremony. Well, as luck had it, the interpreter became ill on the morning of this wedding. I had to wing this one alone.

At the time of the exchange of the rings, the best man found that the two rings had slipped into each other and they could not be separated. I asked the altar server to get a knife. There I was by the altar, trying to separate the two rings. I could tell from the couple's expressions that they thought this was all part of the ceremony in America. They smiled through it all. So if you ever attend a Vietnamese wedding and they are trying to separate the wedding rings with a knife, remember where the tradition began!

"The fear of the Lord will gladden the heart:giving happiness and a crown of joyfulness".

—Book of Eccesiasticus

Anthony F. Rigoli, O.M.I.

AN INTERESTING BAPTISM

So many wonderful memories always return to me of my days at St. Jude's Church in Sumter, South Carolina. I remember one very warm and humid Sunday. It was the baptism of a baby after our last Mass. The baby was crying. It was, of course, feeding time. Well, Mom decided to feed the baby during the ceremony. That seemed like a natural thing to do. And natural it was! She was breast-feeding the baby; however, when it came time for me to anoint the baby's forehead, I decided it would be better to skip this part of the ceremony. Discretion is needed at times!

*"I have told you this so that my joy may be
in you and your joy complete."*

— *Gospel of John*

Anthony F. Rigoli, O.M.I.

WHERE'S THE ICU

A story that has always made me realize the power of God happened again while I was in South Carolina. I had just returned that evening from visiting my family in California. The plane landed in Columbia, South Carolina and I was about forty-five minutes away from getting back to the rectory. When I arrived at the rectory, a parishioner was waiting for me in the driveway. She had asked me if I had seen Mr. McMahon who was doing poorly at the VA Hospital back in Columbia. She told me she would drive me back to Columbia because she knew the family was there and needed me.

Honestly, having just finished a six-hour plane trip and the ride back from Columbia, I wasn't too eager to go back, but she drove me. When we arrived at the hospital, she dropped me off at the front entrance so she could park the car. When I entered the hospital, there was no one at the reception desk. I didn't know where to find Mr. McMahon. All of a sudden, out of nowhere, a young Afro-American man appeared. He asked if I was the chaplain. I said, 'No',but wondered if I could help him. He told me that a man who had helped him and his family years ago was in the ICU and could I go and say a prayer for him. I told him I would, but he never gave me his name, but rather led me to the Intensive Care Unit. I told him I had to see someone and would return to bring him in to see his friend. When I got into the unit, the family was present around Mr. McMahon. As I was anointing him, he died peacefully. The children all said, "Father, we are so grateful you came. We had been praying for the Lord to give us a sign that Dad would now be in peace. Your presence verified our prayers."

I then went back out into the waiting room to find the young man who wanted me to pray for his friend, but I could not find him. He seemed to have vanished.

After the funeral, a week later, I went to visit Mrs. McMahon. As I was visiting, for some strange reason, I made a comment about the beautiful fireplace they had in the living room. She then proceeded to tell me that Mr. McMahon would probably never want anyone to know, but when their children were attending St. Anne's School, there was a poor family down the road for whom Mr. McMahon had paid their tuition to attend St.Anne's. In gratitude, their father built the fireplace for the McMahon's. It was a masterpiece.

All of a sudden, it hit me…the young man at the hospital! Could he have been from this family? Could he have been an angel? No Coincidence!

Anthony F. Rigoli, O.M.I.

"Shout for joy, you heavens, for, Yahweh has been at work."

——*Isaiah*

THREE TO GET MARRIED

Performing a wedding for a newly-ordained priest is always an experience. I recall one of my first weddings. The parish was a very large parish with plenty of weddings for any new priest to get a lot of experience. Since this was one of my first weddings, I went and bought a wedding cross (a cross joined by two rings in the center) . My theme was that Christ was the center of this marriage. I began very emphatically, "Today, there are not two present for this marriage but three." Naturally, I meant the Lord. I could tell by my introduction to the homily that some were a bit aghast. I had totally forgotten that the young bride was pregnant. I did retrieve myself by immediately showing the wedding cross, and explaining that Jesus was the Third and Most Important member of the marriage. You could actually feel and see the sigh of relief on everyone's face. I have never used that homily again.

Anthony F. Rigoli, O.M.I.

"Clap your hands, you people, acclaim God with shouts of joy."

——Psalm 47

FRED'S LARGE FUNERAL

I spent two years in Watervliet, New York. At that time, I was the Vocation Director for my community, the Oblates of Mary Immaculate. We had a House of Studies there. Since I was not attached to any parish, many pastors would call us for assistance. On one particular morning, I received a call from one of the pastors in a neighboring parish. He was not feeling well and had a funeral coming in within the hour. He asked if I could take the funeral for him. He, himself, didn't know the man who died. He only told me that he had served our country in the Army.

When the funeral began, the church was practically full. I had almost forgotten the man's name except that I had written it on a piece of paper I had in my pocket. His name was Fred.

Thinking that this man certainly was loved by so many who came to his funeral, I gave quite a homily on what a tribute it was to Fred that so many would be here today. Many must have loved him. I went on and on and made him look like one of Mother Teresa's best friends.

At the cemetery, after the committal at the grave, one of his sons came over to thank me. He said, "Father, I want to thank you for having the funeral for my Dad, but I must tell you that we are really at peace now that he is gone. You see, he really wasn't very nice to our Mom and the reason there were so many in the church today was that we just discovered that he had another family in another part of the State. This was the first time we all met".

I am sure that both wives must have wondered, "who is that priest talking about? surely, it is not our Fred!!!" Never again will I give a homily for a funeral unless I know something about the person. Lesson well learned!!!

"The secret of a happy life is the moderation of our pleasures in exchange for an increase of joy."

——Bishop Fulton J. Sheen

TRAVELING WITH MOM

As I mentioned in my introduction, my Mom suffered from Alzheimer's for about six years. She was the happiest person I ever met. A great lesson that I learned from her was to enjoy the present moment. Most of us spend most of life worrying about the past or worrying about the future. My Mom, because of her condition, never remembered the past and she certainly didn't think about the future. But, boy, she did enjoy the present moment. No matter if it was taking a ride in the car, having ice cream, going to a birthday party with family, each moment was enjoyed to its fullest. She would ask me every day, "Is it my birthday today?" I would always answer, "Yes", and go for ice cream with her. Today, I try to enjoy the present moment. It is a way of keeping Mom in my heart.

An interesting story was that every year I would take Mom to visit my brother in California. Mom had lived there for around fifteen years with Dad. She had many friends there so she looked forward to the trip each year. One thing that made the trip difficult over the years was, as her Alzheimer's became more profound, she would have to use the ladies' room at the airport. Naturally, I couldn't go in with her, but I would scan the crowd for some woman with a friendly face, and ask if she would be so kind as to go in with her.

Well, on the last trip we made, we were in the Pittsburgh Airport. Mom said she needed the bathroom. I looked around and saw two friendly-looking women. I asked them if one of them would be so kind as to accompany Mom. The women said they would be honored. When she took off with one of them, the other woman asked me if I knew who I was just talking with, and she proceeded to tell me that they were both going to a conference on Alzheimer's and the woman who had accompanied Mom was one of the main speakers. When she returned with Mom, she told me that I made her day. She said that it was people like Mom that made her love her work. This certainly was not a coincidence. I guess God had a sense of humor at that moment.

Anthony F. Rigoli, O.M.I.

"Man is the only creature endowed with the power of laughter."

——*Greville*

THE FUNERAL

S ome of my experiences were not always humorous, but as I see it, they were very providential. God has had His Hand in each moment of my life.

When I was in Buffalo, at St. Rose's, I received a telephone call from dear friends whose son, Matthew, I had baptized when he was a baby. They had moved to a town outside of Atlanta, Georgia. The call was very sad. They were calling to tell me that Matthew, along with another young boy, had been in an accident and had died. They asked if I could be with them at the funeral.

Since it was Friday and the funeral would be on Monday, I knew I had to work pretty hard to change a few appointments and try to get a ticket on an airplane to Atlanta. The funeral was in Atlanta on Monday at eleven in the morning.

Delta had a flight that left at seven in the morning and arrived by ten. They were going to pick me up at the airport. It was cutting it close but it was the only flight I knew could get me there.

That Monday morning I arrived very early at the airport in Buffalo only to discover that the Delta flight was canceled. I called the family to tell them I would see if I could find another flight, but it didn't seem hopeful. I told them not to come to the airport. I didn't want anyone to miss the funeral. Thank God, their pastor was there for them.

As I was going down the gates, I discovered another airline, AirTran. They were in the process of loading the plane for Atlanta. I asked the ticket taker if I could exchange my Delta ticket. She was so accommodating and gracious. She even said she would call the family in Atlanta to tell them I would still be there. When I boarded the plane, I thought to myself, what am I doing? I don't even know where the church is located and how am I going to get there? I am so terrible with directions.

As I entered the plane, an old friend from my neighborhood spotted me. He asked me where I was going. I told him I was heading to the funeral of a young boy. He was aware of the accident since he had seen it in the Atlanta papers. He told me his office was right near the church and he had a car at the airport. He would get me to the church. I arrived five minutes before the Funeral Mass was to begin. The family, in the midst of their pain, had a sign that God was giving them some comfort during this most tragic moment. I know it was God watching me and making sure I was present to this family.

Definition of the word: JOY

J O Y =   *Jesus*

                   Others

                   You

Anthony F. Rigoli, O.M.I.

DOES HE KNOW WE ARE COMING

As I have mentioned my Mom suffered from Alzhiemer's. She, however, always left us with smiles and good laughs. On one occasion one of her closest cousins died. Phil used to visit her weekly and always brought donuts. I could always tell if he had been there by the donuts.

When Phil died I wasn't sure if I would tell Mom. However, she always enjoyed being with the family. I decided to take her to the wake. She would be able to be with so many of her cousins. We were always a very close family.

On the way to the funeral home, I kept on reminding Mom of Phil's death and that we were going to pay our respects. She seemed very much at peace and content to be going. When we arrived at the funeral home, some of the family were outside. Mom said loudly:"Do you think Phil knows that we are coming?" Well, she brought the house down. I am sure that cousin PHil also had a smile on his face from heaven.

"I've Got that Joy, Joy, Joy Joy down in my heart"

Anthony F. Rigoli, O.M.I.

LOOK, MOM, IT'S GOD!

There was a family in Our Lady of Guadalupe Church here in New Orleans that had a small child. Whenever they would come to Church the mother would always tell the child to be quiet in Church because it is God's House and people are praying to Him. Whenever this family left the church after Mass, I would always acknowledge how well-behaved their children are in church.

One day I happened to be shopping in Walmart's, unbeknown to me this family was also in the store. Well, when their little son saw me, he blirted out…."Look, Mom, it's God"! I felt very honored to be identified with God. I don't know if God felt the same!

"The fear of God is glory and pride and happiness and a crown of joyfulness"

—Ecclesiasticus

Anthony F. Rigoli, O.M.I.

HAIRCUTS BY THE PADRE

When I entered the seminary, one day a notice appeared on the bulletin board. The notice read: "Anyone able to cut hair, please sign below". No one signed the notice. Well, the next day, the notice read: "Anyone ever see someone cut hair, please sign below". Well, I certainly could sign this notice. That was the beginning of my 'career' as a barber for the seminary. As the years went by I took my trade to nursing homes as well as hospitals where patients were unable to get out to have their hair cut. I met some of the nicest and most interesting people.

Later, when I was chaplain at D'Youville College in Buffalo, New York, I had a sign: "Haircuts by the Padre"-all proceeds go towards the shelter for the homeless! Well as students and some faculty came in my office for a haircut, I had the best conversations. When you have someone in a barber chair where they can not move, you have lots of conversation.

To this day, I really believe that signing that notice way back in the seminary, really opened up so many doors to meeting new people.

"I bring good tidings of great joy, a joy to be shared by the whole people"

Anthony F. Rigoli, O.M.I.

STILL ON MY WAY TO HEAVEN!

I began this short book sometime ago. I had to put it on hold due to illness. Yes, on the way to heaven, we often have to pause because of sickness. Last September, I faced surgery for prostate cancer. It was to be a simple operation and I had no fears going into surgery. Well, two hours into the operation, I had a heart attack. If you are going to have one, the best place is on an operating table in the hospital. The surgeon was able to get a heart surgeon to come in and put a stent into my artery which was 100% blocked.

The next morning, when I awoke in ICU I knew something didn't seem right. The surgeon came in to tell me they couldn't remove the cancer due to the heart attack. I would later be given radiation.

All that is now in the past. I feel terrific and my health is better than ever. Again, I met so many people during those forty days of radiation as well as during cardiac rehab. I also learned to enjoy each day fully.

Today, I enjoy good health and am most grateful to my family and many friends for their prayers. It just wasn't my time and there is still more funny things to happen on my way to Heaven!!!!!

About the Author

Father Anthony F. Rigoli is a member of the Oblates of Mary Immaculate. Born in Buffalo, New York, he was ordained to the priesthood in 1972. He has served in parishes in Harrisburg, Pa., Indianapolis, IN., Sumter, S. C. and in Buffalo, New York. Besides parish work, he served as Vocation Director for his community and also taught high school. He has served as Campus Minister at D'Youville College and chaplain to Holy Angels Academy in Buffalo, New York. At present, he is pastoral associate at Our Lady of Guadalupe Church in New Orleans, La. and chaplain at Our Lady of Holy Cross College.

Printed in the United States
29155LVS00001B/28-93